Study Guide for Decoding Midsummer Night's Dream

With Typical Questions and Answers

Steven Smith

Sherwood Press

CONTENTS

— • —

How to use this guide

This analysis of William Shakespeare's "Midsummer Night's Dream" intends to offer a study guide to readers who need a more in-depth view of the story.

This book is divided into questions, so the answers appear in a short essay style and may include repeated information. The questions are typical of what a high school student may experience.

I want to think all important questions have been either directly or indirectly answered. However, if you, the reader, feel something is missing, please reach out to me, and I will add it!

Happy studying!

Steven Smith

stevensmithvo@gmail.com

www.classicbooksexplained.com

—•—

Historical background to William Shakespeare

William Shakespeare, often regarded as the greatest writer in the English language and the world's pre-eminent dramatist, was born in 1564 in Stratford-upon-Avon, England. The exact date of his birth is not known, but it is traditionally observed on April 23, Saint George's Day.

Shakespeare's father, John Shakespeare, was a glove-maker and a local political figure. His mother, Mary Arden, was the daughter of a prosperous landowning farmer. Shakespeare had two older sisters and three younger brothers.

He likely attended the King's New School, a free chartered grammar school in Stratford, where he would have studied rhetoric, grammar, and classics. It was here that he first encountered Latin drama and literature, which had a significant influence on his later works.

At the age of 18, he married Anne Hathaway, a woman eight years his senior. They had three children: Susanna, and twins Hamnet and Judith. Sadly, Hamnet died at the age of 11, an event that is thought to have deeply affected Shakespeare.

In the late 1580s, Shakespeare arrived in London and began his career as an actor and a playwright. By 1592, he had achieved success in both roles, with his plays being produced and performed by several companies.

In 1594, he became a founding member of the Lord Chamberlain's Men, a company of actors. The company was very successful, later becoming the King's Men in 1603 when King James I ascended the throne and became the company's patron. The troupe owned the Globe Theatre and the Blackfriars Theatre, and they produced most of Shakespeare's plays.

Over his 20-year career, Shakespeare wrote about 39 plays, 154 sonnets, and two long narrative poems. His plays cover a range of genres, including histories, tragedies, comedies, and tragicomedies (romances).

Shakespeare retired from public life around 1613 and returned to Stratford-upon-Avon, where he died on April 23, 1616 at the age of 52. Despite his relatively short life, his prolific output and profound influence on literature, drama, and culture have made him one of the most enduring figures in literary history.

—·—

Historical background to William Shakespeare's Midsummer Night's Dream

"A Midsummer Night's Dream" is one of William Shakespeare's most popular and enduring comedies, believed to have been written between 1595 and 1596. The play is set in Athens and consists of several plots that revolve around the marriage of Duke Theseus and the Amazon queen, Hippolyta.

To fully understand the historical context of "A Midsummer Night's Dream", one must consider the wider socio-cultural environment of Elizabethan England (1558-1603), the time period when Shakespeare was writing.

1. **Elizabethan World Order:** The play reflects the Elizabethan worldview and the Great Chain of Being, a hierarchical structure of all matter and life. The chaos caused by the romantic entanglements in the play could be seen as a reflection of what happens when this order is disrupted.

2. **Classical Influence:** The play's setting in Athens, as well as the presence of characters like Theseus and Hippolyta, reflect the Elizabethan England's fascination with ancient Greece and Rome. Theseus, the Duke of Athens, and Hippolyta, the queen of the Amazons, are both figures borrowed from ancient mythology.

3. **Folklore and Superstition:** The character of Puck and the oth-

er fairies can be traced to English folklore and the superstitious beliefs of the time. Fairies were thought to be responsible for various misfortunes and inconveniences, and their interference in the affairs of humans creates much of the play's comedic effect.

4. **Courtly Love and Marriage:** The Elizabethan era had strict norms around courtship and marriage, often arranged for political or economic reasons rather than love. The young lovers in the play rebel against these societal norms, and their pursuit of personal choice may reflect changing attitudes towards marriage during Shakespeare's time.

5. **Theatre in the Elizabethan Era:** Theatre was a growing form of entertainment in the Elizabethan era. "A Midsummer Night's Dream" is self-referential, with a play-within-a-play structure, and satirizes some of the theatrical conventions of the time.

It's important to note that the direct historical influences on "A Midsummer Night's Dream" are not well-documented, making much of this analysis speculative. However, the societal norms, cultural interests, and literary conventions of Shakespeare's time undeniably shaped the way he wrote, and all of these elements are visibly present in "A Midsummer Night's Dream".

Why do students read Midsummer Night's Dream

"A Midsummer Night's Dream" remains a mainstay in school curricula because it is one of William Shakespeare's most accessible and entertaining plays. It offers several points of educational value, including:

1. **Understanding Shakespearean Language and Themes:** Despite being over 400 years old, Shakespeare's work remains relevant because of his profound understanding of human nature and his mastery of the English language. Reading "A Midsummer Night's Dream" exposes students to Elizabethan English, and encourages them to decipher meaning from context, enhancing their language skills. Additionally, the play's themes, including love, dreams versus reality, and the natural versus the supernatural, still resonate with modern audiences and provide fertile ground for discussion.

2. **Exposure to Dramatic Structure and Literary Devices:** The play is a prime example of Shakespeare's skill in structuring a narrative. The intertwining plot lines, mix of comedy and drama, and use of a play-within-a-play offer excellent studies in dramatic structure. "A Midsummer Night's Dream" also includes a range of literary devices such as metaphor, simile, and irony. For instance, when Titania falls in love with Bottom (who has been given a donkey's head), it's an example of dramatic irony - the audience

knows something the characters do not.

3. **Character Analysis and Development:** The characters in "A Midsummer Night's Dream" offer students opportunities to analyze motives, relationships, and character development. Characters like Puck, who serves as a mischievous catalyst for much of the play's action, and the complicated relationships between the four young lovers (Hermia, Lysander, Demetrius, and Helena), are particularly interesting for analysis.

4. **Cultural and Historical Context:** As previously mentioned, the play reflects the societal norms and beliefs of Elizabethan England, from social hierarchy to marriage customs and superstitions about the supernatural. Studying the play provides insight into this historical period.

5. **Discussion of Relevant Social Issues:** While the play reflects the mores of Shakespeare's time, many of its themes remain relevant today. Issues of gender dynamics, personal choice versus societal expectations, and the complexities of love can be explored through the characters' experiences. For instance, Hermia's defiance of her father Egeus' wish for her to marry Demetrius serves as a starting point to discuss individual freedom and choice.

In sum, "A Midsummer Night's Dream" serves as a rich resource for education, with potential for linguistic development, cultural understanding, and critical thinking about enduring social themes.

—•—

Understanding Shakespearean language and themes

Understanding Shakespearean Language and Themes is a crucial part of studying the works of William Shakespeare, one of the most influential figures in English literature. Here's a brief look at each aspect:

Shakespearean Language:

Shakespeare wrote his plays and poems in Early Modern English, which, while recognizable, can seem strange to contemporary readers due to changes in syntax, vocabulary, and pronunciation over time. Understanding Shakespearean language involves several components:

1. **Vocabulary:** Shakespeare's works are renowned for their rich, imaginative vocabulary. He used words that have since fallen out of use, and he coined many words and phrases that are still in use today. Understanding these words often requires use of a glossary or footnotes.

2. **Syntax and Grammar:** Shakespeare often used unusual word order to achieve a certain rhythm or rhyme, or to emphasize a particular word. Understanding this "inverted" syntax can be challenging but is crucial to comprehending the meaning of Shakespeare's lines.

3. **Verse and Prose:** Much of Shakespeare's dialogue is written in verse, particularly iambic pentameter, a rhythmic pattern that

consists of five pairs of unstressed and stressed syllables. Recognizing this pattern can aid in understanding and appreciating Shakespeare's skill as a writer.

4. **Figurative Language:** Shakespeare frequently used metaphors, similes, puns, and other forms of figurative language. Understanding these requires both knowledge of the language of Shakespeare's time and the ability to interpret symbolic language.

Shakespearean Themes:

Shakespeare's works explore a wide array of themes, many of which remain relevant today. Here are a few major themes commonly found in his works:

1. **Power and Ambition:** Many of Shakespeare's works, such as "Macbeth" or "King Lear," explore the effects of power, ambition, and political intrigue on individuals and societies.

2. **Love and Relationships:** Shakespeare frequently examined various aspects of love, including romantic love, familial love, and friendship. "A Midsummer Night's Dream," for example, explores the irrationality of love and the complications of relationships.

3. **Identity and Deception:** The theme of characters disguising their true identities, or being deceived by others, is prevalent throughout Shakespeare's works. This theme often serves to drive the plot and add complexity to the characters.

4. **Fate and Free Will:** Shakespeare's works often question the extent to which individuals control their own destinies. This theme is particularly evident in plays like "Romeo and Juliet," where the protagonists are said to be "star-crossed" lovers.

5. **Nature vs. Supernatural:** Many of Shakespeare's works, includ-

ing "A Midsummer Night's Dream," explore the boundaries between the natural world and the supernatural or mystical.

Understanding Shakespearean language and themes allows readers to appreciate the depth and complexity of his works, and provides insights into the human condition that remain relevant even in modern times.

Exposure to dramatic structure and literary devices

"A Midsummer Night's Dream" is a quintessential example of Shakespeare's skill in dramatic structure and use of literary devices, and studying it can greatly enhance one's understanding of these areas.

Dramatic Structure:

1. **Multiple Plot Lines:** The play intertwines several stories, including the lovers' entanglements, the fairy king and queen's spat, and the amateur actors' attempts to put on a play. These plots collide and interact with each other, providing a rich and layered narrative structure that keeps the audience engaged.

2. **Play within a Play:** "A Midsummer Night's Dream" uses a play-within-a-play structure, with the characters of the "Mechanicals" (a group of amateur actors) rehearsing and performing the play "Pyramus and Thisbe." This offers an opportunity to explore the idea of performance in literature and the line between reality and fiction.

3. **Three-Act Structure:** The traditional three-act structure (setup, confrontation, and resolution) is also evident in "A Midsummer Night's Dream." The setup introduces the characters and their initial conflicts; the confrontation occurs in the enchanted forest, where the conflicts are exacerbated, and the resolution occurs

when the characters return to Athens, and the conflicts are re-solved.

Literary Devices:

1. **Dramatic Irony:** This is a technique where the audience knows something the characters do not. For instance, when Puck applies the love potion to Lysander's eyes, causing him to fall in love with Helena instead of Hermia, the audience is aware of this mix-up, but the characters are not.

2. **Metaphor and Simile:** Shakespeare uses metaphor and simile throughout his works to provide vivid descriptions and to make comparisons. In "A Midsummer Night's Dream," for example, Helena describes her love for Demetrius saying, "Your wrongs do set a scandal on my sex. / We cannot fight for love as men may do. / We should be wooed and were not made to woo" (Act II, Scene 1). This compares the societal expectations of gender roles in love and courtship.

3. **Foreshadowing:** This technique is used to hint at future events. For example, the confusion and mischief that ensue after Puck's application of the love potion is foreshadowed when Oberon describes the flower's magical properties.

4. **Puns:** Shakespeare frequently uses puns (play on words) for comedic effect. For instance, the character Bottom, who is transformed into a donkey, is a pun on the word "ass" (another term for donkey), reflecting both his physical transformation and the foolishness of his character.

Studying "A Midsummer Night's Dream" can offer a wealth of insights into Shakespeare's command of dramatic structure and literary devices, providing a model of effective and engaging storytelling.

—·—

CHARACTER ANALYSIS AND DEVELOPMENT

"A Midsummer Night's Dream" is filled with a range of complex and interesting characters, each of whom undergoes some form of development throughout the play.

Hermia: Hermia begins the play in a position of conflict, wanting to marry Lysander but being forced by her father to marry Demetrius. Hermia's character showcases her bravery, determination, and independence, as she defies societal norms and expectations to pursue her own desires. Her decision to elope with Lysander to the forest initiates the primary plot of the play.

Lysander: Lysander's love for Hermia is steadfast at the beginning of the play, but the application of the love potion changes his affections to Helena. This showcases the theme of love's fickleness. However, once the potion's effects are reversed, he returns to being the dedicated lover, demonstrating the theme of resolution and reconciliation.

Demetrius: Initially, Demetrius is in love with Hermia but used to be a suitor of Helena. The love potion causes him to fall back in love with Helena, which remains even after the potion wears off. His character transformation shows the unpredictable and often inexplicable nature of love.

Helena: Helena starts as a character scorned in love, desperate for Demetrius's affection. She feels slighted and humiliated, especially when she believes that the other three lovers are mocking her in the forest.

However, by the end, she finds happiness with Demetrius, underscoring the play's theme of resolution.

Oberon and Titania: As the King and Queen of the Fairies, their conflict over a changeling boy causes the mischief in the fairy world to spill over into the human world. Oberon's trick on Titania causes her to fall in love with Bottom (who has been given a donkey's head), and Oberon himself orchestrates the love-potion confusion among the young Athenian lovers. This exhibits their capricious and powerful natures. However, after Oberon has made his point, they reconcile, demonstrating the theme of resolution and unity.

Puck (Robin Goodfellow): Puck serves as the catalyst for much of the play's action. His mischievous nature and mistakes with the love potion result in much of the confusion and humor in the play. Despite the chaos he causes, he ends the play on a note of peace and goodwill, suggesting that all the mischief was in good fun.

Bottom: Bottom provides comic relief in the play. His transformation into a donkey and the subsequent enchantment of Titania is a source of humor. Despite his ridiculousness, his overconfidence, and his unwitting involvement in the fairy world, Bottom has a good heart and is a dedicated actor in the "Pyramus and Thisbe" play.

Each character in "A Midsummer Night's Dream" provides an opportunity for deep analysis and understanding of human nature, motivations, and the complexities of relationships. Their individual journeys and transformations drive the action of the play and contribute to its enduring appeal.

—·—

Cultural and historical context

"A Midsummer Night's Dream" reflects the culture and history of the time it was written in, the late 16th century. Here are some key aspects that pertain to the cultural and historical context:

1. **Elizabethan World Order:** In Elizabethan times, the world was believed to have a specific order – the Great Chain of Being – which was a hierarchical structure of all matter and life. When this order was disrupted, chaos ensued. This is reflected in the play when the fairy world interferes with the human world, causing a disruption that leads to confusion and conflict.

2. **Mythology and Folklore:** The setting of the play in ancient Athens and the inclusion of characters such as Theseus and Hippolyta show the influence of classical mythology, which was revered in Elizabethan times. Furthermore, the use of fairies and magic in the plot represents popular English folklore and superstitions of the time.

3. **Elizabethan Theatre:** During the Elizabethan era, theatre became a popular form of entertainment, and "A Midsummer Night's Dream" self-referentially explores this with the 'play within a play' structure. The Mechanicals' preparation and performance of the "Pyramus and Thisbe" play satirizes some of the theatrical conventions of the time.

4. **Elizabethan Views on Love and Marriage:** The play explores various dimensions of love, many of which were contentious in Elizabethan society. The notion of marrying for love was not universally accepted, and marriages were often arranged for social or financial reasons. Hermia's refusal to marry the man her father has chosen for her reflects a rebellion against this tradition.

5. **Midsummer Eve:** The title of the play and much of its action reference Midsummer Eve (the summer solstice), traditionally a time of magic and mystery, which would have been an important part of the cultural calendar in Elizabethan England.

6. **Gender Roles:** The play also explores gender roles in a way that was both reflective of and challenging to the norms of the time. For example, the submissive role expected of women is both upheld (Hippolyta's submission to Theseus) and challenged (Hermia's rebellion against her father's will).

By understanding these cultural and historical contexts, we can gain a deeper appreciation of "A Midsummer Night's Dream" and the ways in which Shakespeare was both a product of his time and a revolutionary writer who challenged societal norms.

—·—

Discussion of relevant social issues

"A Midsummer Night's Dream" might have been written over four centuries ago, but it touches upon social issues that are still relevant in modern society. Here are some examples:

1. **Consent and Agency**: Hermia's father, Egeus, insists that she marry Demetrius, despite her wishes to marry Lysander. This raises issues of consent and personal agency, especially in regard to arranged marriages and the rights of women to choose their own spouses. Today, these issues remain relevant as discussions about women's rights and autonomy continue globally.

2. **Gender Roles**: The play challenges traditional gender roles in various ways. For example, Helena's pursuit of Demetrius, although depicted comically, reverses traditional gender roles in courtship. Titania, as a powerful queen who initially refuses to yield to her husband Oberon's demands, also defies gender norms of the time. This offers a basis for discussion on how gender roles have evolved over time and how they continue to be challenged today.

3. **Power Dynamics**: Power dynamics are at play throughout the entire narrative - between the lovers, the fairies, and the "Mechanicals". Oberon and Titania's struggle for control over a changeling boy, for example, can be seen as a commentary on the use and

abuse of power. In modern times, issues of power dynamics are ever-present, from personal relationships to politics.

4. **Class Distinctions**: The play also comments on social stratification and class. This is evident in the stark differences between the Athenian nobles and the "Mechanicals" or the working class. The ridiculed performance of "Pyramus and Thisbe" by the Mechanicals could be interpreted as a satirical commentary on class distinctions and the elitism of high culture. This discussion remains pertinent in current times where social inequality and class consciousness are prevalent issues.

5. **Reality vs. Illusion**: The play delves into the contrast between what is real and what is imagined or perceived, a theme that is highly relevant in the digital age, where the boundaries between reality and virtual spaces have become increasingly blurred.

Through discussing these social issues as they are presented in "A Midsummer Night's Dream", students can gain a more profound understanding of the timeless relevance of literature and its reflection on societal norms and challenges.

— • —

Summary of the Play

"A Midsummer Night's Dream" is a comedy play by William Shakespeare, believed to have been written between 1590 and 1596. The play is set in Athens and consists of several subplots that revolve around the marriage of Theseus, the Duke of Athens, and Hippolyta, the former queen of the Amazons. These subplots involve love, misunderstanding, transformation, and a play within a play.

Act 1:

Egeus, a nobleman, comes before Duke Theseus with his daughter Hermia, who is in love with Lysander. Egeus wants Hermia to marry Demetrius, whom he has chosen for her, but Hermia refuses, preferring Lysander. Theseus declares that Hermia must obey her father or face a penalty of death or becoming a nun. Lysander and Hermia plan to elope and confide in Helena, Hermia's friend who is in love with Demetrius. Helena decides to tell Demetrius in hope of winning his affection.

Meanwhile, a group of Athenian craftsmen, the "Mechanicals," are rehearsing a play "Pyramus and Thisbe" to perform at Theseus's wedding.

Act 2:

In the fairy world, King Oberon is quarrelling with his Queen Titania over a changeling boy she refuses to give him. Oberon instructs his servant Puck to fetch a magical flower, the juice of which can make someone fall in love with the first creature they see upon waking. He plans to use it on Titania.

Demetrius and Helena are in the same woods. Oberon, seeing Demetrius reject Helena, orders Puck to put the flower's juice on Demetrius's eyes, but Puck mistakenly applies it to Lysander, who falls in love with Helena.

Act 3:

Puck transforms one of the Mechanicals, Bottom, by giving him a donkey's head. The transformed Bottom encounters the enchanted Titania, who, affected by the flower's juice, falls in love with him.

Realizing his mistake with the flower, Puck puts the potion on Demetrius's eyes, who then falls in love with Helena. Now both Lysander and Demetrius are pursuing Helena while Hermia is left out.

Act 4:

Oberon obtains the changeling boy from the enchanted Titania and then releases her from the spell. She is horrified by what has happened.

Oberon instructs Puck to fix the love chaos in the mortals. Puck applies the antidote to Lysander's eyes, so when they all wake, Demetrius loves Helena, and Lysander loves Hermia. Theseus finds the lovers in the forest and, hearing their changed affections overrules Egeus and allows the lovers to marry in pairs as they wish.

Act 5:

At Theseus and Hippolyta's wedding, the Mechanicals perform "Pyramus and Thisbe," providing comic relief. Afterwards, the lovers retire to their chambers. Puck and Oberon bless the marriages, promising they will be free of contention and sorrow. Puck ends the play by asking the audience for applause if they enjoyed the performance.

The play ends with Puck's famous lines: "If we shadows have offended, Think but this, and all is mended: That you have but slumbered here, While these visions did appear..."

"A Midsummer Night's Dream" is a vibrant comedy that intertwines multiple narratives, blurs the lines between illusion and reality, and explores themes such as love, power, and transformation.

ACT I

Act 1, Scene 1:

The play opens in Athens at the court of Duke Theseus. The Duke is preparing for his wedding to Hippolyta, the Queen of the Amazons. Their nuptial is only four days away, and Theseus is impatient for the time to pass.

Their discussion is interrupted by Egeus, who enters the scene with his daughter Hermia and two young men, Lysander and Demetrius. Egeus is asking for the Duke's intervention because Hermia, despite her father's wishes, refuses to marry Demetrius and declares her love for Lysander instead. Egeus invokes an old Athenian law that allows a father to either force his daughter to marry the man of his choice or have her put to death. Duke Theseus gives Hermia until his wedding day to make a choice: obey her father, face death, or enter a nunnery.

After the Duke and others exit, Lysander and Hermia plan to elope. They decide to meet in the woods outside Athens the following night and then to proceed to the home of Lysander's widowed aunt, far from Athenian law, where they will marry.

Helena, who is in love with Demetrius, enters the scene. Hermia tells Helena about her plan to elope with Lysander. In a bid to win Demetrius's favor, Helena decides she will betray her friend's secret and tell Demetrius of Hermia and Lysander's plan to elope.

Act 1, Scene 2:

The second scene introduces a group of Athenian craftsmen (the "Mechanicals") planning to perform a play at the Duke's wedding celebration. Peter Quince, a carpenter, is trying to organize the group and assign roles for their play, "Pyramus and Thisbe". Nick Bottom, the weaver, is the most outspoken of the group and is assigned the role of Pyramus. Despite his enthusiasm, Bottom shows himself to be somewhat of a buffoon, offering to play multiple roles and generally making a muddle of the proceedings.

The other roles are distributed among the craftsmen: Flute, the bellows-mender, is to play Thisbe; Snug, the joiner, is to play the lion; Starveling, the tailor, is assigned to play Thisbe's mother; and Snout, the tinker, will play Pyramus's father. Quince will play Thisbe's father. They agree to secretly meet in the woods the following night to rehearse the play.

—•—

ACT 2

Act 2, Scene 1:

In this scene, the audience is transported from the city of Athens to a nearby forest, the realm of the fairies. The scene begins with a conversation between a Fairy and Puck, also known as Robin Goodfellow. Puck is a mischievous spirit known for his pranks, while the Fairy serves Queen Titania.

Soon after, Oberon, the King of the Fairies, arrives with his servant Puck. Oberon and his wife Titania have been quarreling over a young Indian prince whom Titania has adopted; Oberon wants the boy as his page, but Titania refuses. After Titania leaves, Oberon decides to play a trick on her to get the boy. He sends Puck to get a magic flower called 'love-in-idleness.' The juice of this flower, when applied to a person's eyelids while they sleep, makes them fall in love with the first living thing they see upon waking.

Meanwhile, Helena, who is in unrequited love with Demetrius, pursues him into the forest. Oberon, unseen by the humans, overhears Demetrius rejecting Helena and feels sorry for her. He orders Puck to use the juice of the flower on Demetrius when he is asleep so that he will love Helena when he wakes up.

Act 2, Scene 2:

In this scene, Titania instructs her fairies to sing her to sleep and protect her from the creatures of the forest. Once Titania falls asleep, Oberon steals in and squeezes the juice of the 'love-in-idleness' on her eyelids, hoping that she will wake to fall in love with some vile creature. He anticipates that while she's distracted, he can then convince her to give him the Indian boy.

Meanwhile, Lysander and Hermia, who have decided to elope, decide to rest in the forest for the night. Puck, searching for the Athenian man Oberon spoke of earlier (meaning Demetrius), stumbles upon the sleeping Lysander and mistakes him for Demetrius. He applies the love juice to Lysander's eyes.

Afterward, Helena chases Demetrius into the area and wakes Lysander while trying to determine whether he knows where Demetrius has gone. Upon waking, Lysander sees Helena first and falls in love with her due to the effect of the potion. This leaves Hermia abandoned when Helena, thinking Lysander is mocking her, leaves with Lysander following her.

— · —

ACT 3

Act 3, Scene 1:

In the forest, the group of amateur actors, the Mechanicals, gather to practice their play, "Pyramus and Thisbe," for the Duke's wedding celebration. Bottom, the weaver, continues to overstep his role, making absurd suggestions about how to improve the play.

Puck happens upon the group and decides to have some fun. He transforms Bottom's head into that of a donkey while he's off-stage, and when Bottom returns to the rehearsal, his fellow craftsmen are terrified by his appearance and run away. Despite his new appearance, Bottom is oblivious and believes that his friends are attempting to play a joke on him.

Meanwhile, Titania, who has been enchanted by Oberon with the juice of the 'love-in-idleness' flower, wakes up and sees Bottom with the donkey's head. As intended by Oberon's plan, she falls madly in love with him and orders her fairy attendants to wait on him and make him comfortable.

Act 3, Scene 2:

In another part of the forest, Puck reports back to Oberon, mistakenly thinking that he has successfully completed Oberon's orders. However, when Hermia and Demetrius come by, arguing, Oberon realizes that Puck has applied the potion to the eyes of the wrong Athenian man. Oberon then directs Puck to remedy his mistake by anointing the eyes of Demetrius.

Helena, chased by the love-stricken Lysander, also arrives in the area. Demetrius, still in love with Hermia, wants nothing to do with Helena, but Puck fixes this by applying the potion to Demetrius's eyes while he sleeps. When he awakes, he sees Helena, and under the potion's influence, immediately falls in love with her.

Now both Lysander and Demetrius are in love with Helena, much to her disbelief. She thinks they are mocking her, while Hermia can't believe that Lysander has stopped loving her. This leads to a quarrel between Hermia and Helena, and the two men also become confrontational. Puck enjoys the confusion he has caused but eventually, under Oberon's orders, leads the men away from each other and makes them sleep. He then applies a remedy to Lysander's eyes to correct his earlier mistake, so that Lysander will love Hermia again when he wakes.

In the meantime, Oberon releases Titania from her spell and takes the Indian boy from her. With everything put right in the fairy world, Oberon and Titania reconcile and decide to bless Theseus's marriage with their presence.

ACT 4

Act 4, Scene 1:

At the beginning of this scene, Titania and Bottom, still with his donkey's head, are deeply in love (due to the effect of the love potion). Titania treats Bottom as a nobleman, and he is waited upon by her fairy attendants. Meanwhile, Oberon discusses with Puck how his plan has been successful.

When Titania falls asleep, Oberon takes the opportunity to reverse the love spell on Titania, revealing that he's now obtained the changeling boy. Upon waking, Titania is horrified by the sight of Bottom, and she and Oberon reconcile, leaving to join in the fairy revels. Puck then removes the donkey's head from Bottom, who wakes up thinking he has experienced a strange dream.

In another part of the forest, Theseus, Hippolyta, Egeus, and their hunting party discover the four young Athenians (Lysander, Hermia, Demetrius, and Helena) asleep. Upon waking, all the love entanglements have sorted themselves out: Demetrius loves Helena, and Lysander loves Hermia. Egeus is initially upset, but Theseus overrules Egeus's demands and proposes a group wedding. They all return to Athens to prepare for the weddings, leaving the confused lovers to ponder what they believe to have been a dream.

Act 4, Scene 2:

This scene takes us back to Athens, where the group of Mechanicals is worried about the missing Bottom and fear they will have to cancel their play without him. Their relief is immense when Bottom returns, and they hurry off to get ready for their performance of "Pyramus and Thisbe" at Theseus's wedding celebration.

—•—

ACT 5

Act 5, Scene 1:

This scene begins back in Athens, where Theseus, Hippolyta, and the lovers are discussing the strange events of the previous night. The couples can barely remember the magical happenings in the forest, and they regard their experiences as dream-like.

After their discussion, the group prepares to watch the play "Pyramus and Thisbe," performed by the Mechanicals, as part of the wedding festivities. The performance is comically bad due to the actors' over-the-top performances and numerous mistakes, but the noble spectators are good-natured about it. They laugh and joke about the absurdities of the performance, but they also appreciate the effort the workers have put into their play.

After the play ends, Theseus and Hippolyta retire for the night, followed by the newlywed couples. Once the palace is empty of mortals, Puck enters to sweep the threshold, a traditional task that symbolizes clearing away bad luck.

Oberon and Titania then enter with their fairy court. They have reconciled their differences and are ready to bless the palace and its inhabitants. They perform a fairy dance around the stage and then exit.

Puck, remaining on the empty stage, delivers the final lines of the play, a direct address to the audience. He explains that if the play has offended, they should remember it as nothing more than a dream. He asks for the audience's applause, and the play ends.

MAIN CHARACTERS

"A Midsummer Night's Dream" is full of fascinating characters. Here are the main characters:

1. **Theseus**: He is the Duke of Athens who is preparing to marry Hippolyta, the Queen of the Amazons. Theseus represents power and order throughout the play.

2. **Hippolyta**: She is the Queen of the Amazons who is about to marry Theseus. Like Theseus, she is a symbol of order, but she's also an example of a powerful woman who becomes submissive to her husband.

3. **Hermia**: She is in love with Lysander and a good friend to Helena. However, Hermia's father Egeus wants her to marry Demetrius. She is strong-willed and determined to marry for love, not according to her father's wishes.

4. **Lysander**: He is in love with Hermia and they plan to elope. He is a character who values love over law.

5. **Demetrius**: He was engaged to Helena, but breaks off their engagement to pursue Hermia. He represents the fickleness of love.

6. **Helena**: She is in love with Demetrius, despite his cruel treatment of her. She signifies the agony of unrequited love.

7. **Oberon**: The king of the fairies, who is engaged in a feud with his wife, Titania, over a changeling boy. He's a symbol of mischief due to his love for playing tricks.

8. **Titania**: Queen of the fairies, who refuses to give Oberon the changeling boy, causing conflict. She falls in love with Bottom (who has been given a donkey's head) due to a love potion.

9. **Puck (Robin Goodfellow)**: Oberon's servant, who is mischievous and loves to play tricks. He is responsible for the mix-ups and confusion with the love potion.

10. **Nick Bottom**: An overconfident weaver chosen to play Pyramus in a play that a group of craftsmen (the Mechanicals) are performing for Theseus's wedding. His character embodies comic relief. After Puck transforms his head into that of a donkey, he is unwittingly ensnared in the fairy world when Titania falls in love with him.

DESCRIBE THESEUS

Theseus is the Duke of Athens in "A Midsummer Night's Dream," and he represents order, rationality, and power throughout the play.

1. **Authority and Rationality**: Theseus is a figure of authority, both due to his position as the Duke of Athens and his character's rational nature. This is displayed at the very beginning of the play when Egeus comes to him for help, complaining that his daughter Hermia refuses to marry Demetrius, the man Egeus has chosen for her, and instead desires to marry Lysander. Theseus upholds the Athenian law, telling Hermia she must either obey her father, become a nun, or face death (Act 1, Scene 1). However, later, Theseus overrules Egeus and allows the two loving couples to marry whom they wish, demonstrating his ability to make fair decisions (Act 4, Scene 1).

2. **Love and Marriage**: Theseus is engaged to Hippolyta, the queen of the Amazons. Throughout the play, he looks forward to his wedding with excitement and anticipation. Their relationship is not without its complexities; in the play's opening, Theseus mentions that he won Hippolyta's love "with my sword," suggesting their union might be the result of conquest rather than mutual affection (Act 1, Scene 1). Nevertheless, in their interactions, they show mutual respect and affection.

3. **Enjoyment of Entertainment**: Theseus appreciates the effort made by the craftsmen in their play "Pyramus and Thisbe," despite its comic ineptitude. He defends their intentions and watches the play with good humor (Act 5, Scene 1).

4. **Contrast to the Fairy World**: Theseus's rationality and his grounding in the mortal world contrast with the dreamlike, magical world of the fairies. In Act 5, Scene 1, Theseus dismisses the lovers' account of the previous night's events in the forest, attributing their experiences to their imaginations, and preferring to see the world through a rational lens.

Through these characteristics and actions, Theseus embodies an authority figure who is rational, powerful, but also understanding and fair.

DESCRIBE HIPPOLYTA

Hippolyta is the Queen of the Amazons, engaged to Theseus, the Duke of Athens, in "A Midsummer Night's Dream". She is a somewhat less prominent character than Theseus but represents power, honor, and a certain degree of independence and strength, though she is also depicted as submissive to Theseus.

1. **Power and Honor**: In Greek mythology, the Amazons were a race of warrior women known for their courage and pride, and Hippolyta was their queen. Although Shakespeare doesn't depict Hippolyta as a warrior in "A Midsummer Night's Dream", her royal status and her Amazonian background hint at her authority and strength.

2. **Marriage to Theseus**: The play begins with the upcoming nuptials of Hippolyta and Theseus. Hippolyta is marrying Theseus because he has won her in battle (Act 1, Scene 1), an arrangement that could suggest a lack of agency on her part. However, she doesn't express any opposition to the marriage, suggesting either contentment with or resignation to her situation.

3. **Submissiveness**: Though Hippolyta is a queen in her own right, she is generally deferential to Theseus throughout the play. She doesn't challenge his authority and mainly serves to affirm and support his decisions. This could reflect the traditional gender

roles and power dynamics of the time.

4. **Insight and Perception**: Hippolyta is not without her insights. In Act 5, Scene 1, she's more willing than Theseus to believe that there might be truth in the lovers' story of their magical experiences in the forest. Where Theseus sees the story as more of a fantastical tale, Hippolyta suggests that "all the story of the night told over, / And all their minds transfigured so together, / More witnesseth than fancy's images, / And grows to something of great constancy" (Act 5, Scene 1), showing her perceptiveness and open-mindedness.

While Hippolyta's role is somewhat secondary, her character subtly represents a dignified and perceptive woman who navigates the complexities of her situation with grace.

Describe Hermia

Hermia is one of the central characters in "A Midsummer Night's Dream". She's a young woman from Athens who is bold, passionate, and steadfastly in love with Lysander, despite her father's wishes for her to marry another man, Demetrius.

1. **Passionate Love**: Hermia is deeply in love with Lysander and is willing to defy the Athenian law and her father, Egeus, to be with him. In Act 1, Scene 1, she says to Lysander, "My good Lysander! / I swear to thee, by Cupid's strongest bow, / By his best arrow with the golden head..." Here, she swears by the gods of love that she will be true to him.

2. **Determined and Defiant**: Hermia is prepared to go to great lengths for love. She chooses to flee Athens with Lysander to escape the law that forces her to either marry Demetrius, become a nun, or die. She says, "I will yield my virgin patent up / Unto his lordship, whose unwished yoke / My soul consents not to give sovereignty." (Act 1, Scene 1). This shows her defiance and strength of will.

3. **Jealousy**: When Puck, the fairy, mistakenly anoints Lysander's eyes with the love potion, causing him to fall in love with Helena, Hermia becomes fiercely jealous. This demonstrates her passionate nature and ability to stand up for herself.

4. **Friendship**: Hermia's relationship with Helena is also a key aspect of her character. They are best friends, although their friendship becomes strained due to the love triangle with Demetrius and Lysander. However, by the end of the play, after all the mix-ups are resolved, their friendship appears to be restored.

In summary, Hermia embodies the theme of passionate, rebellious love in "A Midsummer Night's Dream". She's determined to follow her heart, even when it leads to conflict and confusion.

DESCRIBE LYSANDER

Lysander is a young nobleman from Athens in "A Midsummer Night's Dream". He's in love with Hermia, and she reciprocates his feelings, but their path to union is blocked by Hermia's father Egeus, who wants her to marry Demetrius instead.

1. **Passionate Love**: Lysander's love for Hermia is one of his defining characteristics. He's willing to defy Athenian law and risk everything to be with her. In Act 1, Scene 1, he tells Hermia, "I will my Hermia. Helena, I love thee; / By my life, I do; / I swear by that which I will lose for thee, / To prove him false that says I love thee not."

2. **Defiance and Cunning**: When Egeus forbids him from marrying Hermia, Lysander doesn't despair or give up. Instead, he devises a plan for the two of them to elope, showing his determination and resourcefulness.

3. **Affected by Puck's Potion**: Lysander becomes a key figure in the play's comedic misunderstandings when Puck, a fairy, mistakenly anoints his eyes with a love potion while he sleeps. When Lysander wakes up, he sees Helena and falls in love with her. This causes much confusion and heartache until Puck finally corrects his mistake.

4. **Resolution and Love Rekindled**: After waking from a sec-

ond enchanted sleep—this time with the love spell correctly applied—Lysander's love for Hermia is restored. In the end, he marries Hermia, and they reconcile with Demetrius and Helena, showing a resolution to the chaotic events.

In summary, Lysander is a determined, resourceful, and passionate character. He represents the power of love and the lengths one will go to overcome obstacles in its path. His experiences with the love potion also contribute significantly to the play's humor and plot complications.

DESCRIBE DEMETRIUS

Demetrius is another young nobleman from Athens in "A Midsummer Night's Dream". He is initially favored by Hermia's father, Egeus, to marry Hermia, despite the fact that Demetrius once courted Hermia's friend Helena, who is still in love with him.

1. **Fickle in Love**: Demetrius starts the play having deserted Helena, with whom he was previously in love, to court Hermia, showing his fickle nature. Helena reminds him of his change of heart in Act 1, Scene 1, saying, "I must confess, I have heard so much, / And with Demetrius thought to have spoke thereof; / But, being over-full of self-affairs, / My mind did lose it."

2. **Chosen Suitor**: Egeus favors Demetrius to be Hermia's husband, leading to a complex love triangle between Hermia, Lysander, and Demetrius. However, Demetrius's insistence on marrying Hermia seems more focused on his rivalry with Lysander than on his love for Hermia.

3. **Affected by Puck's Potion**: Demetrius becomes a critical figure in the comedic misunderstandings of the play when Puck, at Oberon's instruction, anoints his eyes with a love potion. Upon waking, Demetrius sees Helena and falls in love with her again.

4. **Resolution and Love Rekindled**: Demetrius's love for Helena remains even after the other magical mishaps are resolved, sug-

gesting that the love potion simply served to restore his original affection for her. By the end, Demetrius and Helena reconcile and prepare to marry alongside Hermia and Lysander, leading to a happy ending.

In summary, Demetrius's character provides a great deal of the conflict and resolution in "A Midsummer Night's Dream". His shifting affections, under the influence of Puck's love potion, contribute significantly to the comedic misunderstandings and, ultimately, to the joyful conclusion of the play.

—•—

DESCRIBE HELENA

Helena is a young woman from Athens in "A Midsummer Night's Dream". She was once the beloved of Demetrius, who has since shifted his affection to Hermia. Helena, however, remains deeply in love with Demetrius, and this unrequited love defines much of her character and actions in the play.

1. **Unrequited Love**: Helena's enduring love for Demetrius, despite his harsh rejection, is a central part of her character. In Act 1, Scene 1, she declares, "I am your spaniel; and, Demetrius, / The more you beat me, I will fawn on you." These lines show the depth of her feelings and the pain she endures from his rejection.

2. **Betrayal of Friendship**: In her desperation to regain Demetrius's affection, Helena betrays her friendship with Hermia by revealing to Demetrius Hermia's plan to elope with Lysander. This act of desperation shows the extent to which her unrequited love has driven her.

3. **Mistaken Affection**: Helena becomes the object of both Lysander's and Demetrius's affections after Puck misuses the love potion. However, she believes their declarations of love are part of a cruel joke, highlighting her self-doubt and insecurities.

4. **Resolution and Love Returned**: After the magical confusion is resolved, Demetrius's love for Helena remains, suggesting that

the love potion helped him rediscover his genuine feelings for her. Helena's love is finally reciprocated, and she marries Demetrius in a quadruple wedding with Hermia and Lysander, and Theseus and Hippolyta.

In summary, Helena is a character driven by her unrequited love for Demetrius. She's willing to risk her closest friendship to regain his affections. Despite her insecurities and heartache, she provides some of the most comedic moments in the play. Ultimately, her story offers a hopeful ending, showing that love can overcome rejection and misunderstandings.

Describe Oberon

Oberon is the King of the Fairies in "A Midsummer Night's Dream". He is powerful, proud, and a bit mischievous, and his conflict with his wife, Titania, over a changeling boy sets much of the play's action in motion.

1. **Marital Conflict**: Oberon's main conflict in the play is with his wife, Titania, over who should have possession of a changeling boy. He is stubborn and proud, refusing to back down and eventually resorting to magical means to get his way. This conflict leads to much of the mischief and mix-ups in the story.

2. **Power and Command**: As the King of the Fairies, Oberon has significant power, both in terms of his authority over the other fairies and his magical abilities. He is able to order Puck to fetch the love potion and to correct his mistake later on. He's also able to enchant Titania to fall in love with the first creature she sees, leading to the comic subplot of her falling for Bottom, who has been given the head of a donkey.

3. **Use of Magic**: Oberon is instrumental in creating the play's confusion and comedy through his use of the magical love potion. His instruction to Puck to anoint the eyes of the "Athenian man" leads to both Lysander and Demetrius falling in love with Helena. Despite the chaos this causes, Oberon seems to enjoy the results.

4. **Resolution and Reconciliation**: Despite his quarrels and mis-

chief, Oberon is also capable of resolving conflicts. When he re-alizes the distress caused by his actions, he takes steps to correct the course of events. He also eventually reconciles with Titania, suggesting a capacity for forgiveness and understanding.

In summary, Oberon is a dynamic character who, despite his initial portrayal as stubborn and somewhat mischievous, shows growth and re-sponsibility throughout the course of the play. He is central to both the main plot and the subplot, using his power and magic to both complicate and ultimately resolve the story's conflicts.

—◦—

Describe Titania

Titania is the Queen of the Fairies in "A Midsummer Night's Dream". She is strong-willed, dignified, and loving, but she finds herself at odds with her husband, Oberon, over the custody of a changeling boy, which becomes a central conflict in the play.

1. **Marital Conflict**: At the beginning of the play, Titania and Oberon are engaged in a feud over a changeling boy Titania has adopted. Titania refuses to give the boy to Oberon, which showcases her protective and maternal qualities, as well as her defiance and independence.

2. **Love for the Changeling Boy**: Titania's affection for the changeling boy is not only the root of her conflict with Oberon, but also illustrates her compassionate nature. She cares for the boy as her own, having promised his deceased mother—a devotee of hers—that she would guard him.

3. **Enchantment and Love for Bottom**: Oberon, in an act of revenge, puts a spell on Titania that makes her fall in love with the first creature she sees upon waking up. This turns out to be Nick Bottom, an actor whose head has been magically transformed into that of a donkey's by Puck. Her doting on Bottom, despite his grotesque appearance, adds a layer of comedy to the play and highlights the irrationality and capriciousness of love.

4. **Reconciliation with Oberon**: Eventually, Oberon removes the spell and Titania wakes up, no longer in love with Bottom. Upon reconciling with Oberon, she agrees to let Oberon have the changeling boy, resolving their conflict and restoring balance in their realm.

In summary, Titania's character embodies themes of love, maternal affection, and conflict. Despite her dispute with Oberon, she is not depicted as a villain but rather as a strong-willed queen who can be both tender and fierce. Her enchantment and subsequent infatuation with Bottom contribute significantly to the play's humor and theme of love's unpredictability.

Describe Puck (Robin Goodfellow)

Puck, also known as Robin Goodfellow, is a central character in "A Midsummer Night's Dream". He is a mischievous fairy and serves as Oberon's jester and right-hand man. Puck's actions, especially his mistakes, create many of the play's most comedic and chaotic moments.

1. **Mischief and Pranks**: Puck is known for his trickery and enjoys causing harmless trouble. He is delighted by the confusion his actions cause among the humans. As he proudly states in Act 2, Scene 1, "I am that merry wanderer of the night."

2. **Magic and Mistakes**: Puck is responsible for many of the magical mishaps in the play. After Oberon instructs him to apply the love potion to the eyes of the "Athenian man" (meaning Demetrius), Puck mistakenly applies it to Lysander, leading to a series of love triangles and miscommunications. He also transforms Bottom's head into that of a donkey, causing Titania to fall in love with him.

3. **Oberon's Servant**: Puck serves Oberon and carries out his orders throughout the play, although not always accurately. Despite his mistakes, Puck remains loyal to Oberon and works to rectify the problems he creates.

4. **Narrative Role**: As the character who directly addresses the audience in the play's epilogue, Puck serves as a bridge between the magical world of the play and the real world of the audience. He

asks the audience to forgive any offenses and to appreciate the play as if it were a dream.

In summary, Puck is the catalyst for much of the play's action, and his antics introduce both comedy and chaos. As a symbol of mischief and disorder, he contrasts with the orderliness of the human world, embodying the play's exploration of the clash between reality and illusion, order and disorder, and the rational and irrational.

DESCRIBE NICK BOTTOM

Nick Bottom is a character in "A Midsummer Night's Dream" who provides much of the play's humor. He is a weaver by trade but is also part of an amateur group of actors preparing a play for Duke Theseus's wedding. He is boisterous, confident, and somewhat foolish, traits that make him one of the most memorable characters in the play.

1. **Aspiring Actor**: Bottom is enthusiastic and ambitious about his role in the play "Pyramus and Thisbe", which the amateur actors are preparing for Theseus's wedding. He desires to play all the roles, a comical display of his overconfidence and lack of self-awareness. In Act 1, Scene 2, he asserts, "Let me play the lion too: I will roar, that I will do any man's heart good to hear me."

2. **Transformation into an Ass**: Puck, finding the rehearsal of the actors amusing, decides to play a trick on Bottom and transforms his head into that of a donkey's. Bottom, unaware of his transformation, continues to act as normal, which creates a lot of humor.

3. **Titania's Love Interest**: While transformed, Bottom encounters Titania, who, under the influence of Oberon's love potion, falls deeply in love with him. Despite his grotesque appearance, Titania dotes on him and has her fairies attend to him.

4. **Unfazed by the Extraordinary**: Even after his peculiar experience in the forest and being loved by the Fairy Queen, Bottom re-

mains unfazed. When he awakes (with his human head restored), he simply assumes he has had a strange dream. His inability to grasp the extraordinary events that have happened to him is both amusing and endearing.

In summary, Nick Bottom, with his overconfidence and lack of self-awareness, provides much of the play's comedic relief. His transformation into an ass and his subsequent love affair with Titania are among the most iconic parts of "A Midsummer Night's Dream".

The most iconic of the main characters

Puck, also known as Robin Goodfellow, is often considered one of the most iconic characters in "A Midsummer Night's Dream," and perhaps in all of Shakespeare's works. As a mischievous fairy and the servant of Oberon, the King of the Fairies, Puck is the character who introduces much of the magic and mischief that sets the plot in motion.

Here are several reasons why Puck is considered iconic:

1. **He drives the plot**: Puck is the one who applies the magic love potion to the eyes of various characters as they sleep, causing them to fall in love with the first creature they see upon waking. This leads to the play's central conflicts and misunderstandings, and the humor that results from these situations.

2. **His mischievous nature**: Puck is a prankster who enjoys causing trouble and watching the chaos unfold. This aspect of his character is best displayed when he deliberately gives Bottom a donkey's head, which leads to the humorous situation of Titania, the Fairy Queen, falling in love with a donkey-headed human.

3. **His relationship with the audience**: Puck often serves as a kind of bridge between the magical elements of the play and the audience. He offers commentary and explanations about the magical events taking place. Most notably, he addresses the audience directly in his famous final monologue, asking for their

applause if they have enjoyed the play and suggesting that they should consider everything they have seen as if it were a dream.

4. **His memorable lines**: Puck has some of the most memorable lines in the play, such as "Lord, what fools these mortals be!" This quote succinctly captures a key theme of the play: the irrationality and foolishness of love.

For these reasons, Puck's character has left a lasting impact on audiences and readers, and he stands as one of the most distinctive characters not only in "A Midsummer Night's Dream," but in the entirety of Shakespeare's canon.

Minor characters

"A Midsummer Night's Dream" features several minor characters who contribute to the richness of the play's narrative. Here are some of them:

1. **Egeus**: Egeus is Hermia's father who insists that she marry Demetrius, even though she loves Lysander. He appeals to Duke Theseus to enforce the law that would allow him to either kill Hermia or send her to a nunnery if she refuses to obey him (Act 1, Scene 1). His insistence sets the lovers' storyline in motion as Hermia and Lysander decide to run away.

2. **The Mechanicals**: Aside from Bottom, there are other "mechanicals" or craftsmen, including Peter Quince, Francis Flute, Tom Snout, Snug, and Robin Starveling. They provide comic relief as they attempt to put on the play "Pyramus and Thisbe" for Theseus's wedding. Their performance in Act 5 is filled with comedic errors, malapropisms, and slapstick humor.

3. **The Fairies**: The fairy world is filled with various minor characters, including Peaseblossom, Cobweb, Moth, and Mustardseed. These are Titania's fairy attendants who are ordered to serve Bottom during Titania's enchantment. Their interactions with Bottom add to the play's humor.

4. **Philostrate**: Philostrate is Theseus's Master of the Revels, responsible for organizing the entertainment for the Duke's wed-

ding. In Act 5, Scene 1, he doubts the quality of the Mechanicals' play, but Theseus decides to watch it regardless, leading to the hilariously disastrous performance.

5. **The Changeling Boy**: Although he never physically appears in the play, the Changeling Boy is the cause of the dispute between Oberon and Titania. He is a young Indian prince that Titania has taken under her care and refuses to give to Oberon, who wants him as his page (Act 2, Scene 1).

These minor characters, though not central to the main plot, add depth and humor to the story and help to advance the plot. They create a richer depiction of both the human and fairy worlds of "A Midsummer Night's Dream".

What are the important relationships

"A Midsummer Night's Dream" has numerous key relationships that drive the narrative and shape the themes of the play. Here are a few of the most significant:

1. **Hermia and Lysander**: Hermia and Lysander are in love at the start of the play, but Hermia's father, Egeus, insists that she marry Demetrius instead. This conflict propels them to run away together into the forest. In Act 1, Scene 1, Lysander tells Hermia, "The course of true love never did run smooth", signaling the challenges they will face.

2. **Hermia and Demetrius**: Demetrius is in love with Hermia and has the approval of Egeus for their marriage. However, Hermia doesn't reciprocate his feelings. His pursuit of Hermia into the forest is a key part of the plot.

3. **Helena and Demetrius**: Helena is in love with Demetrius, but he doesn't return her affections initially. Her unrequited love, and her decision to tell Demetrius about Hermia and Lysander's plan to elope, are major plot points.

4. **Oberon and Titania**: The King and Queen of the fairies are in a disagreement over a changeling boy. This conflict causes Oberon to use a love potion on Titania, leading to comedic and chaotic events. Eventually, they reconcile in Act 4, showing both the con-

flict and reconciliation aspects of relationships.

5. **Titania and Bottom**: The love that Titania, under the influence of the love potion, expresses for Bottom (who has been transformed to have a donkey's head) forms one of the play's most comic and memorable sequences.

6. **Theseus and Hippolyta**: As the Duke of Athens and the Queen of the Amazons, their upcoming wedding sets the stage for the events of the play. Although there's a hint of conflict and tension in their relationship, given that Theseus won Hippolyta in battle, they seem to have found mutual respect and love.

7. **The Mechanicals**: The group of amateur actors, led by Bottom, have a working relationship that provides comic relief. Their efforts to put on the play "Pyramus and Thisbe" lead to humorous misunderstandings and mishaps.

These relationships in "A Midsummer Night's Dream" explore various aspects of love, friendship, authority, and loyalty, creating a complex web of interactions that drive the play's action and themes.

Hermia and Lysander's relationship

Hermia and Lysander's relationship is one of mutual love and affection, albeit filled with obstacles and complications. Their connection is presented as deep and sincere, setting the stage for many of the play's events.

1. **Mutual Love**: In "A Midsummer Night's Dream", Hermia and Lysander are in love with each other from the start. Despite the external pressures and obstacles they face, they are committed to each other. Lysander's words in Act 1, Scene 1, "I will my Hermia", show his determination to be with Hermia despite her father's opposition.

2. **Defiance of Authority**: Hermia's father, Egeus, wants her to marry Demetrius, but Hermia defies this order and chooses to be with Lysander. This rebellion against parental authority and societal expectations is a significant aspect of their relationship. Hermia boldly tells her father in Act 1, Scene 1, "I would my father looked but with my eyes", expressing her wish that her father could see Lysander through her eyes.

3. **Escape to the Forest**: To escape the laws of Athens and Egeus's control, they decide to run away together to Lysander's aunt's house where they can marry without needing her father's consent. This plan, introduced by Lysander in Act 1, Scene 1, sets the primary action of the play in motion.

4. **Magical Interference and Misunderstandings**: Their relationship becomes complicated when Puck, under Oberon's order, mistakenly applies the love potion to Lysander's eyes, causing him to fall in love with Helena. This creates a series of comedic and chaotic events in the forest.

5. **Restoration of Love**: Eventually, Puck rectifies his mistake and Lysander's love for Hermia is restored. In the end, they are allowed to marry each other, establishing a happy ending for their relationship.

Overall, Hermia and Lysander's relationship is a central focus in "A Midsummer Night's Dream". Their struggle against societal expectations and their unwavering love for each other are key themes that are explored through their relationship.

HERMIA AND DEMETRIUS' RELATIONSHIP

Hermia and Demetrius's relationship in "A Midsummer Night's Dream" is complicated and one-sided at the beginning of the play. Demetrius is in love with Hermia and has the approval of Hermia's father, Egeus, to marry her. However, Hermia does not reciprocate his feelings and is in love with Lysander. The relationship undergoes significant change as the play progresses.

1. **Arranged Marriage**: The play begins with Egeus insisting that Hermia marry Demetrius. He brings the matter to Duke Theseus, demanding that the law be enforced that would compel Hermia to obey his wishes or face severe consequences (Act 1, Scene 1). Despite her father's insistence and the societal expectation, Hermia refuses to comply, showing her independence and commitment to Lysander.

2. **Demetrius's Unreciprocated Love**: Demetrius is in love with Hermia, but she does not return his affection. Demetrius, feeling that he has been slighted by Hermia's love for Lysander, becomes one of the pursuers in the chase sequence in the forest.

3. **Magical Intervention**: Oberon, seeing Helena's distress over Demetrius's rejection of her, orders Puck to apply a love potion to Demetrius's eyes. However, Puck initially mistakes Lysander for Demetrius, leading to further chaos and comedic misunderstand-

ings.

4. **Resolution**: Once Puck corrects his mistake and applies the love potion to Demetrius, he falls in love with Helena, the woman who has been desperately in love with him from the beginning. After this, his pursuit of Hermia ceases, and the couples are properly aligned according to their affections, leading to a harmonious resolution.

In summary, the relationship between Hermia and Demetrius is a key plot driver in "A Midsummer Night's Dream". It evolves from one of forced engagement and unrequited love to a harmonious conclusion as part of the play's exploration of love's complexities.

Helena and Demetrius' relationship

Helena and Demetrius' relationship in "A Midsummer Night's Dream" is complex and undergoes significant development over the course of the play. The relationship begins as unrequited love but evolves into a mutual affection by the end, thanks to some magical intervention.

1. **Unrequited Love**: As the play begins, Helena is desperately in love with Demetrius, who once courted her but now loves Hermia. In Act 1, Scene 1, Helena confesses to Hermia, "How happy some o'er other some can be! Through Athens I am thought as fair as she. But what of that? Demetrius thinks not so", showcasing her sadness and jealousy.

2. **Betrayal and Desperation**: Demetrius's abandonment of Helena to pursue Hermia leaves Helena feeling betrayed and desperate. She is even willing to endure his cruelty, saying in Act 2, Scene 1, "The more you beat me, I will fawn on you. Use me but as your spaniel—spurn me, strike me".

3. **Helena's Plan**: In a desperate attempt to win back Demetrius's affection, Helena tells him about Hermia and Lysander's plan to elope. She hopes this act of loyalty will make him love her again, but it only leads to more chaos and confusion in the forest.

4. **Magical Intervention**: Puck, ordered by Oberon to make Demetrius love Helena, mistakenly applies the love potion to

Lysander first. This results in both Lysander and Demetrius pursuing Helena, much to her confusion and Hermia's dismay. Eventually, Puck corrects his mistake and Demetrius is left in love with Helena, restoring the original pairs.

5. **Mutual Love**: By the end of the play, Demetrius's love for Helena is genuine, thanks to the influence of the love potion. In Act 4, Scene 1, he declares, "To her, my lord, Was I betroth'd ere I saw Hermia. But like in sickness did I loathe this food; But, as in health, come to my natural taste, Now I do wish it, love it, long for it, And will forevermore be true to it."

In conclusion, Helena and Demetrius's relationship evolves from a painful unrequited love to a harmonious union, highlighting the play's theme of love's unpredictability and the magic that can transform relationships.

Oberon and Titania's relationship

Oberon and Titania, the king and queen of the fairies in "A Midsummer Night's Dream", share a tumultuous yet affectionate relationship. Their marital strife and subsequent reconciliation serve as one of the key plot developments in the play.

1. **Marital Conflict**: As the play begins, Oberon and Titania are in the midst of a heated disagreement over a changeling boy. Titania refuses to give the boy to Oberon, which angers him. This marital strife has dramatic effects, causing chaos in the natural world, as noted in Act 2, Scene 1 when Titania says, "The ox hath therefore stretch'd his yoke in vain, The ploughman lost his sweat, and the green corn Hath rotted ere his youth attained a beard".

2. **Manipulation and Revenge**: In retaliation, Oberon decides to use a love potion on Titania, making her fall in love with the first creature she sees upon waking. He hopes this will distract her so that he can take the changeling boy. This plot leads to one of the play's most famous comedic moments when Titania wakes to see Bottom, who has been given a donkey's head by Puck, and falls deeply in love with him.

3. **Titania's Enchantment**: Under the influence of the love potion, Titania dotes on Bottom and treats him as a beloved. This represents a playful, yet somewhat humiliating, punishment for her

defiance.

4. **Reconciliation**: After Oberon obtains the changeling boy, he feels remorse for his actions and orders Puck to remove the enchantment from Titania. Upon waking, Titania is horrified by what has transpired but reconciles with Oberon, and they dance and bless the upcoming human marriages together.

Overall, Oberon and Titania's relationship, with its conflicts and eventual reconciliation, reflects the play's exploration of love's irrationality and fickleness. Despite their argument and Oberon's harsh actions, they ultimately reaffirm their love for each other, reflecting the play's theme of resolution and harmony.

Titania and Bottom's relationship

The relationship between Titania and Bottom in "A Midsummer Night's Dream" is a pivotal subplot driven by Oberon's revenge on Titania, adding both comedy and irony to the play.

1. **Enchanted Love**: Titania's affection for Bottom comes as a result of Oberon's magical intervention. Oberon, angry with Titania, orders Puck to squeeze the juice of a love-in-idleness flower onto her eyes while she sleeps. This potion causes her to fall in love with the first creature she sees upon waking. Puck, separately, has placed a donkey's head on Bottom, leading to the comedic scenario where the queen of the fairies is deeply in love with a lowly weaver wearing a donkey's head.

2. **Doting Affection**: Once the enchantment takes effect, Titania dotes on Bottom, showering him with attention and gifts. She summons her fairies to wait on him and is completely smitten, oblivious to his true form. As she says in Act 3, Scene 1, "Come, sit thee down upon this flowery bed, While I thy amiable cheeks do coy, And stick musk-roses in thy sleek smooth head, And kiss thy fair large ears, my gentle joy."

3. **Bottom's Acceptance**: Surprisingly, Bottom accepts Titania's affections and the strange circumstances quite readily. This acceptance adds to the humor of the situation as Bottom seems

unconcerned by the absurdity of his circumstances.

4. **Resolution**: Oberon eventually feels remorse for his trick and reverses the spell. Upon awakening, Titania is appalled by her actions and immediately reconciles with Oberon. Bottom, when he awakens, believes the events to have been a dream, famously stating in Act 4, Scene 1: "I have had a dream, past the wit of man to say what dream it was."

Titania and Bottom's relationship, though brief, serves as a critique of irrational love and societal hierarchy, adding depth to the themes of "A Midsummer Night's Dream". Their interaction also provides comic relief and underscores the absurdity of love that is a key theme in the play.

THESEUS AND HIPPOLYTA'S RELATIONSHIP

Theseus and Hippolyta, in "A Midsummer Night's Dream", represent the ruling class and the authority of Athens. Their relationship serves as a grounding force in the play and contrasts the chaotic events that unfold among the other characters.

1. **Arranged Marriage**: Theseus, the Duke of Athens, is preparing to marry Hippolyta, the Queen of the Amazons. Their union is a result of Theseus defeating Hippolyta's tribe in battle, as referenced in Act 1, Scene 1, when Theseus says, "Hippolyta, I wooed thee with my sword, And won thy love doing thee injuries".

2. **Anticipation of Marriage**: Despite the arranged nature of their relationship, Theseus and Hippolyta show mutual respect and a growing affection for each other. Their wedding serves as the deadline that shapes the plot. In the first scene, Theseus expresses his eagerness for their upcoming wedding day: "Four happy days bring in another moon; but, O, methinks, how slow this old moon wanes!"

3. **Mutual Respect and Authority**: Theseus and Hippolyta's conversations suggest a level of respect and understanding between them. They often discuss the other characters and their predicaments, providing a mature and reasoned perspective. Their roles as Duke and Queen provide a foil to the irrationality and impul-

siveness seen in the young lovers and the fairy king and queen.

4. **Resolution and Celebration**: The play concludes with Theseus and Hippolyta's wedding, bringing together all the characters in a joyful celebration. This serves to tie up all loose ends and emphasizes the themes of reconciliation and unity.

In conclusion, the relationship between Theseus and Hippolyta serves to frame the events of the play, offering a mature and grounded counterpoint to the irrational, chaotic, and passionate relationships of the other characters in "A Midsummer Night's Dream".

—·—

The Mechanicals' relationship

The Mechanicals, also known as the Rude Mechanicals, are a group of common tradesmen in Athens who come together to put on a play ("Pyramus and Thisbe") for the wedding of Duke Theseus and Hippolyta in "A Midsummer Night's Dream". They are not professional actors, which contributes to much of the humor in their scenes. The group consists of Peter Quince, Nick Bottom, Francis Flute, Tom Snout, Snug, and Robin Starveling.

1. **Peter Quince and the Group**: Peter Quince, the carpenter, is the play's organizer and is seen as the leader of the group. He assigns roles, directs the action, and tries to maintain some semblance of order amidst the comical chaos. His relationship with the others is patient and tolerant, even when they show a lack of understanding or skill.

2. **Nick Bottom and the Group**: Nick Bottom, the weaver, is the most enthusiastic and self-assured member of the group, though he is often clueless and overbearing. His relationships with the other Mechanicals is characterized by his dominating personality and desire to play all the roles in the play. The others, however, seem to tolerate Bottom's behavior with good-natured patience.

3. **Collective Camaraderie**: Despite their individual quirks and the comedy of errors that ensue, the Mechanicals display a strong

sense of camaraderie and collective effort. Their shared goal of performing the play for the Duke and his new wife brings them together. Even when Bottom goes missing (due to Puck's prank of transforming his head into that of an ass), they express genuine concern and sadness.

4. **Performance of "Pyramus and Thisbe"**: The highlight of their relationship is the hilariously bad performance of "Pyramus and Thisbe" at the Duke's wedding in Act 5. Their sincere but bumbling efforts, mistakes, and overacting create a bond of humor and shared experience, both among themselves and with the audience.

In conclusion, the Mechanicals' relationship in "A Midsummer Night's Dream" offers comic relief, while also emphasizing the themes of camaraderie, shared effort, and the joy of simple, earnest attempts at creativity, despite the lack of skill or understanding.

—・—

Themes of the play

"A Midsummer Night's Dream" is known for its exploration of several enduring themes:

1. **Love's Complexity**: The play famously examines the various complexities of love, including its irrationality, fickleness, and the conflicts it can cause. The relationship between Hermia and Lysander, Helena and Demetrius, and Oberon and Titania, all portray different facets of romantic love and its complications.

2. **Magic and Transformation**: Magic, mainly through the character of Puck and the love-in-idleness flower, serves as a symbol of the transformative power of love and the unpredictable changes it can bring about. Bottom's transformation into an ass and the shifting affections of the young lovers represent the dramatic and often strange transformations love can cause.

3. **Order and Chaos**: The play contrasts the order and reason of Athens with the magical, chaotic world of the fairies. The confusions and mix-ups in the woods create a chaotic interlude before order is restored with the return to Athens and the marriages at the end.

4. **Dreams and Reality**: The blurred line between dreams and reality is another significant theme. The events of the play are so strange and fantastical that they seem dreamlike, and several

characters question whether they've dreamed the events of the night.

5. **Role of Fate**: The play also explores the theme of fate and free will. While the characters make choices, their lives are also influenced by forces beyond their control, like the fairy magic and the Athenian law.

6. **Nature and the Natural World**: The setting of the play in a forest, and the presence of the fairy world, highlights the theme of nature and the natural world. The fairies are connected to the elements and natural phenomena, and their quarrels have an impact on the natural world, reflecting the connection between the human and natural worlds.

7. **Art and Performance**: Through the performance of the Mechanicals, Shakespeare explores the theme of art, theatre, and performance. The Mechanicals' comically poor performance of "Pyramus and Thisbe" stands in contrast to the "real" drama happening in the woods, suggesting that art is a reflection of life, no matter how imperfect.

8. **Class and Social Hierarchy**: The differences between the noble lovers, the mechanicals, and the fairy king and queen bring out the theme of social hierarchy and class distinctions, showing how love and conflict cut across these societal boundaries.

These themes combine to create a rich tapestry of comedy, romance, and fantasy in "A Midsummer Night's Dream".

DESCRIBE LOVE'S COMPLEXITY

The theme of love's complexity is at the very heart of "A Midsummer Night's Dream," with Shakespeare examining various aspects of love, including its irrationality, fickleness, joy, conflict, and transformative power.

1. **Irrationality of Love**: Shakespeare uses the four young Athenian lovers to show how irrational and unpredictable love can be. Helena is in love with Demetrius who once loved her but now loves Hermia. Hermia loves Lysander and he loves her back, but her father wants her to marry Demetrius. The convoluted love quadrangle becomes even more complex when Puck applies the love potion to the wrong people, causing love to shift rapidly and irrationally.

2. **Transformative Power of Love**: Love is depicted as a force that has the power to transform. This is evident not only in the shifting affections of the four young lovers but also in the enchantment of Titania. Under the influence of the love potion, she falls deeply in love with Bottom, who has been transformed to have a donkey's head, showing how love can make one see beauty where others do not.

3. **Love as a Source of Conflict**: Love is also shown as a source of conflict. Hermia and her father Egeus are at odds over whom she should marry, and this conflict nearly results in severe punishment

for Hermia. Additionally, the initial conflict between Oberon and Titania over the Indian changeling boy is rooted in jealousy and possession, aspects of love that often lead to strife.

4. **Love's Fickleness**: Love's fickleness is portrayed humorously in the play. The use of the love potion results in the lovers' affections changing rapidly, making love seem arbitrary and changeable. Lysander and Demetrius's quick shifts in love from Hermia to Helena and back again exemplify this.

5. **Resolution and Harmony in Love**: Despite the chaos and conflicts caused by love, it eventually brings resolution and harmony. By the end of the play, the correct pairs of lovers are united, Oberon and Titania reconcile, and the overall message is one of love's ultimate power to create harmony.

In conclusion, Shakespeare's "A Midsummer Night's Dream" provides a multifaceted exploration of the complexities of love, making it one of the central themes of the play.

DESCRIBE MAGIC AND TRANSFORMATION

In "A Midsummer Night's Dream", the theme of magic and transformation is pivotal to the development of the plot and characters.

1. **Puck and Fairy Magic**: The character of Puck, also known as Robin Goodfellow, is a mischievous fairy and the main source of magic in the play. His use of a magical flower called "love-in-idleness" to manipulate the affections of the lovers is a key plot device. The effects of the flower are random and chaotic, reflecting the unpredictable nature of love, but also the transformative power of magic itself.

2. **Transformation of Bottom**: Arguably, the most famous transformation in the play is when Puck turns Bottom's head into that of a donkey. This physical transformation underlines the absurdity of the magical events and acts as a humorous element in the play. However, it also brings out the transformative aspect of magic, turning a common man into a creature that becomes the object of the Fairy Queen's affection.

3. **Change in Perception and Reality**: The magic in the play often alters characters' perceptions, blurring the line between illusion and reality. When Titania is enchanted to fall in love with Bottom, she sees him as a beautiful creature, despite his donkey's head. The lovers, too, under the influence of the love potion, perceive their

emotions to have changed, showing how magic can transform perception.

4. **Natural World and Transformation**: The setting of the play in a mystical forest adds to the theme of transformation. The forest is a place where the usual rules do not apply, where fairies interfere in human affairs, and where characters lose and find themselves, transformed by their experiences.

5. **Resolution through Transformation**: It is also through magic and transformation that conflicts are resolved in the play. Puck's magic, despite the initial chaos, eventually leads to the resolution of the love quadrangle among the young Athenians. Moreover, Oberon uses magic to reconcile with Titania.

In conclusion, the theme of magic and transformation in "A Midsummer Night's Dream" is not only central to the play's plot and comedic value, but also serves to underline key aspects of character development, resolution of conflicts, and exploration of love's unpredictability.

DESCRIBE ORDER AND CHAOS

In "A Midsummer Night's Dream," the theme of order and chaos is manifest in the contrasts between the human and fairy worlds, the city of Athens and the nearby forest, and the transformations and mix-ups caused by magic. Here's how the theme unfolds:

1. **Athens versus the Forest**: The orderly world of Athens, with its societal rules and laws, is contrasted with the forest where the fairy world reigns and where norms are often subverted. The strict Athenian law that forces Hermia to choose between death, a nunnery, or marrying a man she doesn't love, exemplifies order. On the other hand, the forest is a place of chaos where magic causes mistaken identities, altered affections, and absurd situations such as Titania, the queen of the fairies, falling in love with Bottom, a man transformed into a donkey.

2. **Human World versus Fairy World**: The human world, represented by the lovers and the mechanicals, is a world of order and reason (despite the personal complications of the lovers), while the fairy world, represented by Oberon, Titania, and Puck, is whimsical and chaotic. The interference of the fairy world in the human world creates a temporary state of disorder and confusion.

3. **Magic as a Source of Chaos**: Puck's misuse of the love potion on Lysander instead of Demetrius, and his transformation of Bot-

tom's head into a donkey's, are instances where magic introduces chaos into the order of human relationships and identities. These magical interferences create a chaotic interlude before order is restored.

4. **Restoration of Order**: By the end of the play, however, order is restored. The lovers are paired correctly with the help of the love potion and return to Athens; Bottom is transformed back into a man and reunites with his fellow mechanicals; and Oberon and Titania reconcile their differences. These resolutions reinstate order in both the human and fairy worlds.

5. **The Mechanicals' Play**: The mechanicals' play "Pyramus and Thisbe," though a chaotic and comically bad performance, also signifies a return to order after the chaotic events of the night. The fact that it is performed in the court of Theseus, in the heart of Athens, further underlines this restoration of order.

The theme of order and chaos in "A Midsummer Night's Dream" serves to emphasize the contrast between societal norms and the unpredictable nature of love, as well as the transition from conflict to resolution, and the ultimate reconciliation of opposites.

—•—

DESCRIBE DREAMS AND REALITY

"A Midsummer Night's Dream" often blurs the line between dreams and reality, and this becomes one of the central themes of the play. Shakespeare uses the characters' experiences and confusions to explore the concept of dreams as both a metaphor for the whims and irrationalities of love and a mechanism to question the nature of reality.

1. **The Enchanted Forest**: The forest, where much of the play takes place, is a dreamlike place where reality is twisted. The fairies' magic, the sudden shifts of love, and the transformations are all so extraordinary that they seem to be products of a dream. When the characters return to Athens, they struggle to reconcile their memories with reality, questioning if what they experienced was a dream or reality.

2. **Love as a Dream**: The irrationality of love is portrayed as dream-like. The effects of the love potion, for instance, are so strange that they are like dreams. When Lysander and Demetrius suddenly change their affections due to Puck's love potion, the switch is so abrupt and irrational that it feels dreamlike. Similarly, when the potion wears off, they 'awaken' to their true feelings, as though from a dream.

3. **Titania's Enchantment**: When Titania is enchanted to fall in love with Bottom, who has the head of a donkey, her perception of

him as a handsome gentleman could be interpreted as a dreamlike state. After the spell is lifted, she reacts as though she is waking from a vivid dream, showing the close relationship between dreams and magical enchantments.

4. **The Lovers' Confusion**: The young lovers, Hermia, Lysander, Demetrius, and Helena, after being subjected to the fairies' magic, are left confused about their experiences. Upon waking, they are uncertain about what has happened, with Demetrius even saying, "Are you sure that we are awake? It seems to me that yet we sleep, we dream." This underscores the dreamlike nature of their experiences in the forest.

5. **Bottom's Dream**: Perhaps the most direct reference to dreams comes from Bottom after he awakes from being transformed, having been the object of Titania's doting affection. He believes he has had a dream "past the wit of man to say what dream it was." He resolves to have Quince write a ballad of this dream, which will be called "Bottom's Dream" because it "hath no bottom."

By using dreams as a metaphor and narrative device, Shakespeare uses "A Midsummer Night's Dream" to explore ideas of perception, reality, and the uncanny experiences of love and desire.

DESCRIBE ROLE OF FATE

In "A Midsummer Night's Dream", the theme of fate plays out in various ways, often intertwined with the themes of love and magic. Here are the ways fate features in the play:

1. **Fate and Forced Love**: The play opens with the situation of Hermia, who is ordered by her father, Egeus, to marry Demetrius, a man she does not love. According to the law of Athens and the will of her father, it is her "fate" to marry Demetrius, demonstrating the power societal structures and parental authority can have over an individual's fate, particularly regarding love and marriage.

2. **Magic and Fate**: The fairy magic, particularly Puck's use of the love potion, is a stand-in for the forces of fate. The characters have no control over their actions once they're under the spell of the potion - Lysander and Demetrius switch their affections, and Titania falls in love with a transformed Bottom. They're all subjected to a fate manipulated by the fairy magic.

3. **Resolution of Love Conflicts**: The resolution of the love quadrangle between Hermia, Lysander, Demetrius, and Helena can also be seen as an orchestration of fate. Despite the confusion and chaos caused by Puck's misapplication of the potion, in the end, the "right" pairs end up together: Lysander with Hermia, and Demetrius with Helena. It seems that despite the mid-play chaos,

fate ensures the "right" lovers unite.

4. **Bottom's Transformation**: Bottom's fate is directly influenced by Puck, who transforms him into a donkey. This results in a series of absurd and comic events, including being adored by the fairy queen, Titania. After the enchantment is lifted, Bottom considers the whole event as a strange dream, suggesting that the weird course of events were beyond his control, thus a work of fate.

5. **Theseus and Hippolyta**: Their relationship suggests the role of fate as well. Theseus won Hippolyta not through a mutual affection but through conquest. However, by the end of the play, they are depicted as a loving couple preparing for their wedding, suggesting that fate may also bring love and happiness in unexpected ways.

The theme of fate in "A Midsummer Night's Dream" thus portrays how unseen forces can manipulate the courses of our lives, particularly in relation to love and relationships, and how chaos can eventually lead to an order that seems "fated".

DESCRIBE NATURE AND THE NATURAL WORLD

In "A Midsummer Night's Dream", the theme of nature and the natural world plays a significant role in shaping the setting, plot, and symbolism of the play. Here are some ways in which this theme manifests:

1. **Setting in the Forest**: The Athenian forest where much of the action takes place is a setting that allows for chaos, magic, transformation, and ultimately resolution. Unlike the city of Athens, which represents order, law, and societal expectations, the forest represents the wild, unpredictable, and free aspects of nature.

2. **Nature as a Source of Magic**: The forest is not just a physical location but also a magical realm inhabited by fairies who possess powers over nature. For instance, Oberon uses a "love-in-idleness" flower, a product of the natural world, to create a love potion that causes the characters to fall in and out of love in seemingly random and chaotic ways.

3. **Contrast between Artifice and Nature**: The play contrasts the world of human artifice (Athens) with the world of nature (the forest). While Athens is ruled by laws and societal norms, the forest is a place where characters can escape these constraints. Hermia and Lysander flee to the forest to escape Athenian law, and it is here that the lovers find their true love matches, suggesting that nature allows for authentic emotions and relationships to

flourish.

4. **Nature and Transformation**: The natural world is a place of transformation in the play. Bottom is transformed into a donkey, the lovers' affections change due to the magical flower's juice, and day turns into night, highlighting nature's mutable, transformative qualities.

5. **Nature Imagery and Symbolism**: Shakespeare uses nature-based imagery and symbolism throughout the play. For example, the moon is often referred to, symbolizing change and transformation. The "love-in-idleness" flower is another major symbol, representing the unpredictable nature of love.

6. **Titania's Speech**: Titania's speech about the upset balance in nature because of her quarrel with Oberon is an essential moment in the play that highlights the connection between the natural world and the fairy world, and how human (or fairy) actions can disrupt nature.

By incorporating the theme of nature and the natural world, Shakespeare emphasizes the unpredictability of love, the dichotomy between societal expectations and personal desires, and the importance of natural balance, all central ideas to the narrative and message of "A Midsummer Night's Dream".

DESCRIBE ART AND PERFORMANCE

The theme of art and performance is central to "A Midsummer Night's Dream," as the play contains within itself another play and comments on the nature of performance, illusion, and interpretation. Here are some ways this theme is explored:

1. **The "Play within a Play"**: The most significant instance of art and performance in "A Midsummer Night's Dream" is the "play within a play" - the "most lamentable comedy and most cruel death of Pyramus and Thisbe." The group of mechanicals, including Bottom, rehearse and perform this play for Theseus and Hippolyta's wedding celebration. This comic performance is not only a source of humor but also provides commentary on the nature of theatricality, performance, and interpretation.

2. **Disguise and Role-playing**: Many characters in the play take on roles or are put into roles unwillingly. Bottom's transformation into a donkey by Puck is one of the most overt instances of role-playing. When Titania falls in love with him, she is essentially falling in love with a character or a façade, not the real Bottom. This highlights how theater and performance can blur the lines between reality and fiction.

3. **The Function of Imagination**: Imagination plays a crucial role in interpreting and creating art, which is reflected in the charac-

ters' experiences. After waking up from their chaotic night in the forest, the lovers wonder if what they experienced was real or just a dream. Theseus even suggests that the lovers, the madman, and the poet are alike in that they all have "seething brains" that shape reality into what they imagine it to be.

4. **Bottom's Dream**: Bottom's dream offers a complex commentary on art and reality. After waking from his enchantment, he believes he has had an "rare vision" and struggles to recount it. His dream, being both part of his reality and a piece of art (since it was designed by Oberon and Puck), blurs the line between life and art, making us question the nature of both.

5. **The Role of the Audience**: The performance of "Pyramus and Thisbe" also comments on the role of the audience in theater. The Athenian nobles watching the play make snide comments and interpret the play as they wish, highlighting that the meaning of a performance can change based on an audience's interpretation.

Through these aspects, "A Midsummer Night's Dream" uses the theme of art and performance to interrogate the nature of reality, illusion, interpretation, and the transformative power of art itself.

DESCRIBE CLASS AND SOCIAL HIERARCHY

The theme of class and social hierarchy is subtly woven into the fabric of "A Midsummer Night's Dream." This theme manifests in a number of ways:

1. **Athens vs. The Forest**: The city of Athens represents the ordered world of society with its rules and hierarchies. Theseus is the Duke of Athens, representing lawful authority. In contrast, the forest is a place where the normal rules and hierarchies of society don't apply. This dichotomy sets the stage for exploring societal norms and their limitations.

2. **Love and Social Expectations**: The conflict in the love story between Hermia, Lysander, Demetrius, and Helena reflects the societal expectations and rules imposed on them. Hermia's father Egeus demands that she marry Demetrius, despite her love for Lysander, insisting on his rights as a father to determine her fate under Athenian law.

3. **Status of Women**: The theme of social hierarchy also surfaces in the portrayal of women in the play. Women, such as Hermia and Hippolyta, are expected to be submissive and obedient to men, reflecting their lower position in the social hierarchy of the time.

4. **Fairy World Hierarchies**: Even in the fairy world, a hierarchy exists. Oberon is the king of the fairies, and Titania is the queen. Puck and the other fairies serve them, showcasing a clear hierarchy.

5. **The Mechanicals**: The group of Athenian craftsmen, known as the mechanicals, represents the lower social class in the play. Their attempt to perform a play for the Duke and Duchess provides comic relief but also highlights their position in society. Their lack of education and refinement, evident in their mispronunciations and misunderstanding of dramatic conventions, contrasts sharply with the nobility's sophistication.

6. **Hippolyta and Theseus**: Their relationship also reflects social hierarchies. Theseus won Hippolyta by defeating her in battle, capturing her, and then deciding to marry her. This power dynamic underscores his dominant position, both in terms of social class and gender roles.

Through these different aspects, "A Midsummer Night's Dream" explores how societal and class hierarchies affect personal relationships, freedom, and the pursuit of love. It also highlights the artificial nature of these hierarchies by presenting a contrast between the ordered world of Athens and the chaotic world of the forest, where traditional social norms are subverted.

Conflicts in the Play

"A Midsummer Night's Dream" is filled with various conflicts that drive the plot, create tension, and contribute to the play's humor. Here are some of the major conflicts:

1. **Love Triangle (or Rectangle)**: At the beginning of the play, there's a complex love conflict between Hermia, Lysander, Demetrius, and Helena. Hermia loves Lysander, but her father, Egeus, wants her to marry Demetrius. Demetrius, who was once engaged to Helena, also desires Hermia, while Helena is still in love with Demetrius. This romantic conflict gets further complicated when Puck mistakenly applies the love potion, leading to more confusion and chaos.

2. **Oberon vs. Titania**: The King and Queen of the fairies are in a dispute over a changeling boy whom Titania has adopted. Oberon wants the boy to become one of his followers, but Titania refuses, leading to a conflict that affects not only their relationship but also the natural world, according to Titania's speech about the upset balance in nature.

3. **Egeus vs. Hermia and Lysander**: Egeus, Hermia's father, wishes to force Hermia into an arranged marriage with Demetrius. However, Hermia is in love with Lysander and wishes to marry him. Egeus takes the matter to Theseus, Duke of Athens, leading to a

societal conflict between parental authority and individual desire.

4. **The Mechanicals and Their Play**: The group of Athenian craftsmen, known as the mechanicals, wish to perform a play called "Pyramus and Thisbe" for Theseus and Hippolyta's wedding. There's considerable comic conflict in their attempts to rehearse the play, particularly as Bottom seeks to play all the parts, and they fret about how to represent various elements without scaring the ladies.

5. **Puck's Mistakes**: Puck, Oberon's mischievous servant, creates conflicts due to his mistakes - he applies the love potion to the wrong Athenian man (Lysander instead of Demetrius), and he transforms Bottom's head into that of an ass, leading to more chaos and confusion.

These conflicts drive the play's plot, contribute to its humor and drama, and allow Shakespeare to explore themes such as the nature of love, the power of magic, societal constraints, and the blurry line between reality and illusion.

LOVE TRIANGLE (OR RECTANGLE) CONFLICT

In "A Midsummer Night's Dream", the complex love rectangle between Hermia, Lysander, Demetrius, and Helena is one of the primary sources of conflict and drama in the play.

At the beginning of the play, Hermia is in love with Lysander, and he loves her in return. Hermia's father, Egeus, however, wants her to marry Demetrius and brings the matter before Theseus, the Duke of Athens, seeking punishment for Hermia if she refuses to obey him (Act 1, Scene 1). Egeus' demand creates a significant societal conflict, pitting the authority of a father and societal norms against the power of love and individual desire.

Demetrius, on the other hand, is the one Hermia's friend Helena loves. Helena's love for Demetrius, who once courted her but now loves Hermia, makes her feel rejected and hopeless (Act 1, Scene 1). She laments her situation, saying, "The more I love, the more he hateth me" (Act 1, Scene 1). Her unrequited love for Demetrius forms a poignant part of the love rectangle's tension.

When Hermia and Lysander plan to run away to get married (Act 1, Scene 1), Helena decides to inform Demetrius about their plans, hoping to win his favor. However, the introduction of the magic love potion by Oberon, the King of the Fairies, adds an extra layer of complexity to the situation. Puck, Oberon's fairy servant, is ordered to use the potion on Demetrius to make him love Helena, but he mistakenly applies it to Lysander's eyes (Act 2, Scene 2). When Lysander awakes, he sees Helena first and falls madly in love with her, leaving Hermia feeling abandoned and confused.

Later, Puck corrects his mistake by enchanting Demetrius to fall in love with Helena (Act 3, Scene 2). Now, both Lysander and Demetrius are pursuing Helena, leading to a comical situation where Helena believes both men are mocking her, and Hermia is heartbroken and angry with Helena.

By the end of the play, Puck reverses the spell on Lysander (Act 4, Scene 1), and the lovers are paired off correctly, with Hermia marrying Lysander and Helena marrying Demetrius, bringing resolution to the love rectangle conflict.

The love rectangle serves to drive much of the play's action, provides humor and tension, and offers an exploration of the themes of love's irrationality and complexity, the impact of external influences on love, and the conflict between personal desire and societal expectations.

OBERON VS. TITANIA CONFLICT

The conflict between Oberon, the King of the Fairies, and Titania, his Queen, serves as a significant subplot in "A Midsummer Night's Dream". The central point of their dispute is over a "little changeling boy" (Act 2, Scene 1) who has come under Titania's protection.

The boy's mother, a devotee of Titania, had died, and Titania wants to raise the boy in honor of her deceased friend. However, Oberon wants the boy for himself, to make him his "henchman" or servant. When Titania refuses to give him the boy, Oberon becomes enraged and decides to humiliate Titania as a form of revenge.

Oberon's plan is to use a magical flower called "love-in-idleness" (Act 2, Scene 1). This flower has been hit by Cupid's arrow and now has the power to make anyone fall in love with the first creature they see upon waking. Oberon orders Puck, his servant, to apply the flower's juice to Titania's eyes while she sleeps, intending to make her fall in love with some vile creature.

When Puck transforms the head of the craftsman, Nick Bottom, into that of a donkey (Act 3, Scene 1), and Titania wakes up to see him (Act 3, Scene 1), she becomes infatuated with him, much to Oberon's amusement. Meanwhile, the conflict between Oberon and Titania is said to have caused disruption in the weather and the seasons, reflecting their influence over the natural world.

Ultimately, after having his fun and getting the boy, Oberon decides to release Titania from the spell. He feels sorry for her and admits he was being revengeful. Puck removes the ass's head from Bottom, and Oberon uses the antidote to the love potion on Titania. When she awakes, she is back in her senses and reconciles with Oberon, ending their conflict (Act 4, Scene 1).

Their conflict explores themes of power, possession, jealousy, revenge, and the ability of love to make people look foolish. This subplot parallels the human lovers' storyline, providing a comparison between mortal and immortal love conflicts and misunderstandings.

Egeus vs. Hermia and Lysander conflict

The conflict between Egeus, Hermia, and Lysander is one of the key conflicts that set the events of "A Midsummer Night's Dream" into motion.
Egeus is Hermia's father, and according to Athenian law, he has the power
to decide whom his daughter should marry. He wishes Hermia to marry
Demetrius, an Athenian gentleman who Egeus believes to be a suitable
match for his daughter (Act 1, Scene 1).

However, Hermia is in love with Lysander, who also loves her. When
Hermia refuses to obey her father's command to marry Demetrius, Egeus
brings the matter to the Duke of Athens, Theseus. Egeus invokes an ancient Athenian law that states a disobedient daughter can be punished by
death or be sent to a nunnery for the rest of her life if she doesn't agree with
her father's decision (Act 1, Scene 1).

Theseus, while empathetic, supports Egeus's right as Hermia's father
and advises Hermia to obey her father. Still, he also gives her time to
consider her choice. He says to her, "Take time to pause; and, by the next
new moon — The sealing-day betwixt my love and me, For everlasting
bond of fellowship — Upon that day either prepare to die For disobedience
to your father's will, Or else to wed Demetrius, as he would" (Act 1, Scene
1).

This confrontation creates a significant societal conflict, pitting the
authority of a father and societal norms against the power of love and
individual desire. Hermia, supported by Lysander, defies this authority by

planning to elope to Lysander's aunt's house, "where the sharp Athenian law cannot pursue" them (Act 1, Scene 1).

Egeus's rigid stand towards his daughter's marriage and Hermia's defiance forms one of the central conflicts in the play and gives a chance for Shakespeare to explore themes of love, autonomy, and societal expectations. The resolution of this conflict comes with the approval of their union by Duke Theseus in the end, following the chaotic events in the forest and the reordering of their love under the influence of the magic potion.

The Mechanicals and Their Play conflict

The "Mechanicals" are a group of amateur actors from the working class in Athens, comprising Peter Quince, Nick Bottom, Francis Flute, Robin Starveling, Tom Snout, and Snug. They plan to perform a play, "Pyramus and Thisbe," for the wedding of Theseus and Hippolyta. Their attempts to rehearse the play, as well as their performance, are a source of much of the comic relief in "A Midsummer Night's Dream."

1. **The Role Assignments**: In Act 1, Scene 2, Peter Quince assigns roles to the rest of the Mechanicals. Nick Bottom, who is a weaver by trade, is eager to play all the parts, causing a great deal of confusion and hilarity. Despite being assigned the role of Pyramus, Bottom wants to play Thisbe, the Lion, and Pyramus all at once. Quince has to keep asserting his authority to keep Bottom in his place.

2. **Rehearsal Challenges**: The group's rehearsals are riddled with misunderstandings about the nature of theater and drama. For instance, they worry that the ladies in the audience will be frightened by the lion and the killing of Pyramus in the play. They decide to explain to the audience that they're not really a lion and that Pyramus isn't really dead, which adds a layer of absurdity to their performance.

3. **Bottom's Transformation**: During a rehearsal in the forest,

Puck transforms Bottom's head into that of a donkey (Act 3, Scene 1). When Bottom returns to the rehearsal, his fellow actors run away in fear, leaving him alone in the forest, where he then encounters the love-potion-affected Titania.

4. **The Performance**: When they finally perform their play in Act 5, it's full of malapropisms, missed cues, and terrible acting, making it hilariously bad. The Athenian nobles watch their performance, making fun of them, but they also appreciate the earnestness of the Mechanicals.

The conflict within the Mechanicals and their play brings a great deal of humor to "A Midsummer Night's Dream" and serves as a form of social commentary. It also speaks to the theme of appearance vs. reality and the transformative power of imagination. Even though they're just simple craftsmen, in their minds and hearts, they're actors putting on a great tragedy.

— • —

WHY IS THIS PLAY A COMEDY

"A Midsummer Night's Dream" is considered a comedy due to its structure, elements of humor, and ultimate happy ending. Here are several reasons why, with references to the play:

1. **Happy Ending**: Like many of Shakespeare's comedies, "A Midsummer Night's Dream" ends happily, with multiple marriages: Theseus and Hippolyta, Lysander and Hermia, and Demetrius and Helena. Even Oberon and Titania reconcile after their dispute. This happy resolution is a standard feature of comedy, which often involves the resolution of conflicts and the restoration of social order.

2. **Humorous Situations and Wordplay**: The play is filled with amusing situations and linguistic humor. For instance, the Mechanicals' attempts to rehearse and perform their play, "Pyramus and Thisbe," are a source of humor. Their misunderstandings about theater, their earnest yet misguided efforts to 'improve' their play, and their final, disastrously bad performance (Act 5, Scene 1) are all comedic elements.

3. **Mistaken Identities and Misunderstandings**: The plot involves multiple cases of mistaken identity, which is a common feature of comedy. For example, Puck mistakenly applies the love potion to Lysander's eyes instead of Demetrius's (Act 2, Scene 2),

causing Lysander to fall in love with Helena instead of Hermia. This leads to a series of comedic misunderstandings and conflicts among the four lovers.

4. **Satire and Parody**: "A Midsummer Night's Dream" contains satirical elements, particularly in its depiction of the Mechanicals and their play. This is a comedic parody of tragic romance, full of malapropisms and absurdities that make the audience laugh.

5. **Elements of the Ridiculous**: The character of Bottom, in particular, provides many moments of comedy. When Puck transforms his head into that of a donkey (Act 3, Scene 1), and he remains completely oblivious, it creates a visual humor that adds to the comedic tone of the play.

In these ways, "A Midsummer Night's Dream" fits the structure and characteristics of a comedy, as it aims to amuse the audience and ends in joy and harmony. The play uses humor, mistaken identity, and elements of the ridiculous to create a light-hearted and entertaining experience for the audience.

—·—

WHAT IS THE CLIMAX OF THE PLAY

In the structure of a classic five-act play, the climax typically occurs near the end of Act 3 or the beginning of Act 4. In "A Midsummer Night's Dream," one could argue that the climax occurs in Act 3, Scene 2, where the confusion and conflict reach their peak before being resolved.

In this scene, all the main characters are in the forest at night, and the confusion caused by Puck's misapplication of the love potion is fully realized. The Athenian lovers - Hermia, Helena, Lysander, and Demetrius - argue and fight. Lysander and Demetrius, both under the influence of the potion, are now in love with Helena, whereas previously both were in love with Hermia. Helena believes she is being mocked, and Hermia is left confused and hurt. The confrontation becomes so heated that Lysander and Demetrius decide to duel over Helena.

Meanwhile, Oberon realizes Puck's mistake and orders him to correct it, leading Puck to lead Lysander and Demetrius on a wild chase around the forest to prevent the duel and tire them out. He then uses the antidote on Lysander, hoping that when all the characters wake, they will be in love with the 'correct' partners.

This scene is the climax because it features the highest level of tension and conflict in the play. It is where all the misapplied magic and mistaken identities come to a head before they start to get resolved in Act 4. The climax provides the turning point that leads towards resolution and the eventual happy ending.

What is the resolution of the play

The resolution of "A Midsummer Night's Dream" is a classic Shakespeare-an comedy ending, with misunderstandings cleared, conflicts resolved, and multiple marriages. Here's a breakdown:

1. **Resolution of the Lovers' Conflicts**: At the beginning of Act 4, Oberon and Puck arrange for the four Athenian lovers to wake up with their love directed to the 'right' people. When they awake, Demetrius is still under the influence of the love potion and now genuinely loves Helena, who happily reciprocates his affection. Lysander's love for Hermia is restored, and they are in love as before. The lovers believe the previous night's events to be a strange dream (Act 4, Scene 1).

2. **Titania and Oberon's Reconciliation**: After Oberon removes the spell from Titania, they reconcile and celebrate their reunion, putting their quarrel behind them (Act 4, Scene 1).

3. **The Mechanicals' Performance**: Bottom returns to Athens and reunites with the other Mechanicals, and they perform their play, "Pyramus and Thisbe," which provides comic relief and enter-tainment at the wedding feast of the three couples (Act 5, Scene 1).

4. **The Marriages**: In Athens, Theseus overrules Egeus's objections and declares that all three couples will be married in a triple

ceremony: Theseus and Hippolyta, Lysander and Hermia, and Demetrius and Helena. The lovers are finally allowed to marry their chosen partners, resolving the conflict that began the play (Act 4, Scene 1).

5. **Puck's Farewell**: The play ends with Puck's monologue. He apologizes if the play has offended the audience and asks them to consider it all just a dream (Act 5, Scene 1).

The resolution, therefore, brings harmony out of chaos, turning discord into accord and allowing love to triumph over all obstacles. The social order is restored, and all the characters find peace and happiness.

What is the moral of the play

"A Midsummer Night's Dream," like many of Shakespeare's plays, doesn't provide a singular, straightforward moral. However, it offers several lessons and insights into human nature and society. Here are a few possible takeaways:

1. **The Complexity and Capriciousness of Love**: The play suggests that love can be a complicated, irrational, and unpredictable force. It doesn't always follow logic or societal rules, and it can lead to conflict and misunderstanding. However, despite its challenges, love can also bring about reconciliation and harmony.

2. **The Power of Dreams and Imagination**: The line between dreams and reality is often blurred in the play, illustrating the power of imagination and its capacity to transform our perceptions. It suggests that reality can be subjective and mutable, and it encourages us to embrace the fantastical and the dreamlike.

3. **The Importance of Balance and Harmony**: Many of the play's conflicts arise from imbalances or disruptions of the natural order, whether it's the discord between Oberon and Titania or the love quadrangle among the four Athenian youths. The resolution of these conflicts and the restoration of harmony underline the importance of balance in relationships and society.

4. **The Absurdity of Pretension and Rigid Social Hierarchies**:

Through the comic subplot involving the Mechanicals and their earnest but misguided attempts to stage a tragedy, Shakespeare satirizes pretensions to grandeur and eloquence. This also serves as a critique of rigid social hierarchies, as the lower-class Mechanicals end up entertaining the aristocratic characters and the audience.

5. **The Power of Nature**: The play frequently references the natural world and its influences, showing both its harmonious aspects and its potential for causing chaos and discord. This reflects the Elizabethan belief in the importance of natural order and the potential consequences of disturbing it.

While the play is fundamentally a comedy designed to entertain, these themes offer deeper reflections on love, society, nature, and the human condition. As always with Shakespeare, the "moral" of the story often depends on the viewer's interpretation.

— · —

Famous lines from the play

"A Midsummer Night's Dream" is full of memorable and quotable lines that have become part of the common lexicon. Here are some of the most famous lines, along with their references:

1. **"The course of true love never did run smooth."** (Act 1, Scene 1)

   ○ This is one of Shakespeare's most quoted lines. Spoken by Lysander to Hermia, it reflects on the difficulties and obstacles that true love often faces.

2. **"Love looks not with the eyes, but with the mind, And therefore is winged Cupid painted blind."** (Act 1, Scene 1)

   ○ Spoken by Helena, this quote reflects the idea that love is a matter of the mind and heart rather than physical appearance, hence the depiction of Cupid as blind.

3. **"Lord, what fools these mortals be!"** (Act 3, Scene 2)

   ○ This line is spoken by Puck, as he watches the Athenian lovers' absurd quarrels and mix-ups. It's a reflection on the foolishness and irrationality of human beings, particularly when they are in love.

4. **"I know a bank where the wild thyme blows, Where oxlips**

and the nodding violet grows." (Act 2, Scene 1)

- Oberon uses these lines to describe the enchanting and magical nature spot where he intends Titania to fall in love with the first creature she sees upon waking.

5. **"And yet, to say the truth, reason and love keep little company together nowadays."** (Act 3, Scene 1)

- Spoken by Bottom, this line echoes the sentiment that love often lacks reason, adding a humorous yet wise observation on the irrationality of love.

6. **"If we shadows have offended, Think but this, and all is mended, That you have but slumbered here While these visions did appear."** (Act 5, Scene 1)

- These lines are part of Puck's final speech to the audience, suggesting that if they did not like the play, they should just consider it a dream.

7. **"Though she be but little, she is fierce!"** (Act 3, Scene 2)

- Spoken by Helena about Hermia, this line is often quoted for its empowering sentiment, even if, in the play, it is part of a tense moment of conflict between the characters.

Each of these quotes reflects key themes in the play, including the nature of love, the contrast between reality and illusion, the power of nature, and the sometimes comical foolishness of human behavior.

www.ingramcontent.com/pod-product-compliance
Lightning Source LLC
Chambersburg PA
CBHW071204120626
46546CB00006B/2413